KEN POUNDERS

BACK FROM THE GRAVE

A JOURNEY FROM DEATH TO DESTINY
THROUGH A RESIDENTIAL DISCIPLESHIP PROGRAM

SEQUEL TO JOURNEY FROM FEAR TO FAITH

BACK FROM THE GRAVE
A Journey From Death To Destiny Through
A Residential Discipleship Program
By Ken Pounders

ISBN: 979-8-9992217-0-4

Prepared for Publication By

B|B
PUBLISHING

MAKING YOUR BOOK A REALITY

Cedar Point, NC | 843-929-8768 | info@BandBpublishingLLC.com

To Contact the Author
PriorityEV.info

CONTENTS

Introduction

KEN & SONYA

Ken Pounders is a missionary evangelist ministering in the U.S., Eastern Europe, Asia, and Central America.

Ken and his wife, Sonya, founded Priority Evangelism in 1998 as a world evangelism training and sending organization. They have devoted themselves to new church planting, missionary evangelism, and Residential Discipleship ministry for forty years. They also direct Outreach Ministries of Alabama, a twelve month residential discipleship program for those overcoming addiction in Valhermoso Springs, AL.

Ken was saved in 1982 from a life of drugs, alcohol, and crime. The Lord opened the door for him to enter OMA (as an alternative to prison) where he was discipled for 13 months. During that time, Ken sensed the Lord's call to take the "good news" of Jesus across the U.S. and around the World.

He began his ministry on the streets, reaching out with the love of Christ outside bars and at rock concerts, teen hangouts, or laundry mats. From those early beginnings, the ministry has grown to have worldwide impact equipping the Church to reach their communities, proclaim the Gospel, and train disciples and leaders around the world.

Ken and Sonya have been married since 1984 and live in Valhermoso Springs, Alabama. They have five grown children and six grandchildren. Ken and Sonya host the Conquer Addiction podcast weekly on all podcast platforms.

Chapter One

A STOLEN LIFE

Have you ever felt like a portion of the timeline of your life was ripped from your grasp? The devil masterfully had a hand in replacing what your life could have been with the trap of poor decisions and regret, and now you feel as if your life is over?

Hello, my name is Ken Pounders, and that is my story. All of my late childhood through my teens years were wasted years, but the story I am about to tell you is not a story to glorify the devil and what he did, but a testimony of the greatness of our God and what He was able to accomplish despite how much I had messed it up.

My story is a story of freedom from addiction. It's a story of life out of death. It's a story of a journey from death to destiny and hopefully a story that can bring hope into your life.

I grew up in a good home, where my parents loved me very much. I had two older sisters that, although I irritated them quite a bit, they cared deeply for me and watched over me carefully–probably too carefully, spoiling me.

I grew up in church. Some people would say that I had a drug problem long before I had a drug problem because my parents drug me to church Sunday morning. They drug me to church Sunday night. They drug me to church Wednesday night, and they drug me to church for revival services.

The only problem was that I never came to a place of having a genuine relationship with Jesus Christ. Even though we were in church, it was more of a ritual to me, and I didn't understand the depths of it.

I remember when I was eleven years old going to the altar in a revival service and praying and receiving Christ, giving my life to Jesus. But even then I didn't understand, and I grew no further.

BAD CHOICES

Over the course of my life, I have learned that all the choices we make, whether good or bad, have effects and consequences. I made some terrible decisions that led to a downward spiral in my life.

At twelve, many of my friend's parents drank. So what did we do? We had the brilliant plan of slipping into their liquor cabinets and refrigerators and siphoning off a little from each bottle. We would also take a few beers out of the fridge, just enough where they wouldn't notice.

We would do this day after day, saving it up, so by the weekend we had enough for a party. We would then go out to a fort we had created in the woods to drink. We thought we were having a great time. I guess we thought we were really grown up.

It wasn't long after that, a friend of mine got his hands on some marijuana. He had never smoked pot, and neither had I. Apparently, his older sister thought he did, because when she owed him some money, she offered to pay him in weed. With my brilliant choice making skills, I chose to accept his offer to try it with him.

To this day, I don't understand exactly why I was so ready for that lifestyle. You would think a twelve or thirteen-year-old boy would have a fear of those things or more common sense. But I wanted to be on the cutting edge of whatever I thought was really happening.

However, all the horrible decisions I was making set the stage for a time of tremendous rebellion in my life. Rebellion against my parents, my teachers, and my church leaders. I was living a life centered on myself, doing what I wanted to do, and how I wanted to do it.

I also wish I could say that all of that was just a phase, but over the next few years, I accelerated out of control.

LIFE IS PRECIOUS

The thief does not come except to steal, and to kill, and to destroy. I have come that they may have life, and that they may have it more abundantly. John 10:10 NKJV

Satan is in the business of stealing life, and mine became prime for the taking.

There is another verse in Proverbs 6 that says an adulteress hunts for the precious life. That passage is talking about literal adultery, but I know that Satan, the enemy of our soul, is always looking to take what is precious to God.

Looking back after decades of ministry, I can think about the many precious people I have met and ministered to, master carpenters, skilled artists, musicians that were unbelievably talented, medical professionals, a veterinarian who had a very successful practice, I have met people from all walks of life that were incredibly gifted and talented yet they fell into some type of trap whether it be drugs, alcohol, sex or many other addictions. People that were precious to God, but the devil was successful in getting their life to spin out of control until they were bound in hopelessness and despair. And that is exactly what happened in my life.

At twelve when I started drinking alcohol, and then using marijuana, the downward spiral continued to taking pills and other drugs.

I had always played sports. I grew up playing basketball, football and running track, and I had always done very well in school. In fact, I was always at the top of my class and I was very popular, even going into junior high school. I was vice-president of my class and everybody liked me, but I started seeing things change in my life.

I lost my interest in sports. Even though I continued to play for a period, it wasn't exciting for me anymore. Then I saw my grades fall. I wasn't interested in studying, and I didn't have the desire to excel in my studies. Then I noticed my friends were changing.

At about the age of fifteen, I realized—though I didn't care—I was no longer just a recreational user, but I had become a full-blown drug addict. It had become a center theme of my life. It was taking control of me and my life was going out of control. And the amazing thing is, it all happened so gradually. I was not an overnight addict. I got to this point in my life step by step, from one awful choice to another.

Chapter Two

IN THE PIT OF DESPAIR

I meet people all the time that wonder, "Is there really a devil who wants to destroy my life?" The answer is a BIG YES, and he wants to put you in a pit.

Do you still not believe me? Then I invite you to come with me as I go to the inner cities of America. Come with me to New Orleans on our annual outreach at Mardi Gras. Come with me to the slums of Freeport, Bahamas were we take teens to minister on the streets. Come with me to Central America, India, and other parts of the world that we minister in and yes, you will discover very quickly that there is a devil, and he wants to destroy people's lives.

I knew it because he was doing that very thing in my life. He was taking me to a place of despair. He was sinking me into a pit, into a hole from which I just could not free myself.

There's a passage of Scripture in Psalms, Chapter 40:1-3, where the psalmist, David, says,

> *I waited patiently for the Lord; and He inclined to me, and heard my cry. 2 He also brought me up out of a horrible pit, out of the miry clay, and set my feet upon a rock, and established my steps. 3 He has put a new song in my mouth—Praise to our God; many will see it and fear, and will trust in the Lord. Psalms 40:1-3 NKJV*

OPPOSITION FROM WITHIN

I understand these words. I understand what the psalmist was talking about. If you look at the context of that passage, you'll discover that David was dealing with struggles from without. He had people that were opposing him. He had people that were attacking him. He had difficulties that he was facing personally.

He was also struggling with opposition from within. He was struggling with sin and with things that were destroying his life. He said, "I found myself in a pit, in a place of despair, in a place of miry clay, a bog, something that I couldn't free myself from."

That is exactly how I felt. As a fifteen-year-old drug addict, I was living to get high, and then with the natural knack of leading others, I led others into the life of addiction as well.

From there, I took the next logical step and went from doing and leading to selling. I mean, if I could buy large amounts of drugs and then sell to my friends at school and on the street, I could make a profit and basically be getting mine for free.

It became a business, a thrill, a passion. It became my life.

On one particular occasion in high school, I scored in the top percentage of the entire nation on the national test we took. When I took the same test the following year, I scored down at the bottom somewhere.

I was so high on drugs that I just took the test as a joke. I went down the page and filled in the little circles however I wanted to. My teachers, my church leaders, and people all around me realized something was wrong.

A GOOD STUDENT

When I was sixteen, I became serious about my studies.

You could say I was a good student, but not in a positive way. After graduating from just using marijuana, I began to use pills that I would find in my parent's cabinet.

So my studies during study hall was with the PDR in the high school library, the Physician's Desk Reference. I read up about different drugs and how they acted in the body and what the recommended dosages were.

Other kids at school realized I was really knowledgeable about the topic. They would bring me drugs they found in their parent's medicine cabinet and ask whether they could get high and how they could use them.

Being the businessman I was, when they brought me their pills and their questions, I would take a percentage of whatever they had.

A DOWNWARD SPIRAL

I sold more and more narcotics at school, and soon I became the biggest drug dealer, not only in my neighborhood, but in my entire high school.

Also at sixteen, I took another bad step. I mainlined narcotics in my veins. I was using everything, LSD, Dilaudid, cocaine, anything I could get my hands on.

Think about the illustration of somebody starting a snowball down a hill. That snowball gets bigger, and as it grows, it becomes a monster. Eventually, the one who is rolling that snowball realizes he is no longer in control and that snowball swallows anything in its course downhill!

That exactly describes what was going on in my life. My drug addiction was speeding up. My selling of narcotics was accelerating. The snowball of my life was rolling faster and faster and I was about to hit a big wall at the bottom of the hill.

One day at my house, me and a friend of mine named Sandy had been getting high all day. After getting restless, I went out to do a little business. I had people I needed to take drugs to, and some that were going to buy.

Even though we were both completely wasted out of our minds, we got into my Volkswagen. I barely made it out of my neighborhood when I came to the first major inter-section. I failed to stop and drove right into the path of a big utility truck that smashed my car into pieces.

It was a miracle that both of us were still alive. She was only slightly injured, and I wasn't injured at all. I remember getting out of the car and wondering what in the world was going on.

Then, the police arrived. They took Sandy home, but when they found narcotics in the vehicle, they took me straight to jail.

I DON'T BELONG HERE

I remember sitting there looking at the walls of that jail cell thinking, "I don't belong here." I grew up in a good upper middle class home. I had everything that I could want.

My parents had told me from the time I was very young that I could become anything I wanted to be. They would send me to college. I had always had my sights on being a veterinarian. It was what was inside me. It was what I really wanted to do. Yet, I found myself sitting in a jail cell.

I was in such denial as well, there were guys in there for all kinds of horrible crimes, there were even two other men in there with me that were long time alcoholics and with all I had done to my life I remember thinking with a condescending attitude, "This is not right, I don't belong here."

Unfortunately, that wasn't the last time I was in jail. Soon after I was released, I was arrested again for drug-related charges. Again, I found myself in that same jail facility.

I was released, and before I knew it, I was arrested again. Over the next two-years, I was arrested on twelve different drug-related charges.

I was in and out of jail so frequently that the last time I

was in, the jailer looked at me as I was being released and he said, *"Ken, we'll see you again in a few days."*

I remember looking at him and I don't know why I said what I said to this day, but I remember looking at him and saying, *"You'll never see me here again. You'll never see me here again unless I'm here preaching the gospel."*

What's so amazing and so ironic about that is that I actually never went back to that jail until years later. Even though that jail facility has been closed down, we received permission from the city managers there in Huntsville, Alabama to go back into that old jail facility.

We were able to film a documentary about my life and what the Lord has done for me. The next time I was in that jail, I actually was sharing the gospel, the good news of what Christ had accomplished in my life.

But let's get back to the story, I remember one day my mom came to visit me in jail and not only was I beginning to feel hopeless and in a pit of despair, but I saw my parents, good people who loved me dearly and were faithful to their church were in the pit with me.

When she came to visit me, she saw into the jail facility where winos and hardened criminals were just lying on the floor. With pain and sadness in her eyes from seeing her son in this condition, she looked at me and said, "Son, that's exactly what you'll become." I laughed at her and said, "I'll never become that." But inside, I knew she was right. Finally, I came to the place where I realized I belonged there. I did fit in.

STILL IN JAIL

When I was released, a friend of mine and his girlfriend picked me up. I sat in his backseat outwardly rejoicing with them because I was no longer incarcerated behind bars, but on the inside I was dying because I was still locked in the cell of my despair.

Outwardly I was trying to laugh. Inwardly I knew I was still an addict and my life had no meaning.

On another day, I remember going to the bathroom and looking at myself in the mirror, knowing I was once very athletic, I had gifts and talents; I had once been popular in high school and now, because of my lifestyle, I was just a skeleton at about 150 pounds with eyes that were dark and sunk back in my head.

With hatred towards myself, I said to the man in the mirror, *"You could have been anything that you wanted to be. But now you're a drug addict."*

A foreboding came over my life, like a black cloud. A deep realization began to sink into my spirit that I wasn't going to live long, and I felt it in my body. I felt like I was dying. I looked like I was dying. I realized at twenty years of age that I would likely never see my twenty-first birthday.

BEHIND THE MASKS

Sometime after that, I had a very surreal moment when I went to a party where all my friends were. Many of them who were at the party were the same people to whom I had sold drugs.

We sat there with loud music playing, getting high and laughing, acting like we're just having a great time. Then I remember looking around and a very strange thing happened. It was like all at once I saw everybody's laughing, smiling mask fall away from their face and behind those masks I saw empty people, I saw fools.

Behind the masks they were crying and hopeless, empty and hurting. As I looked around, I thought to myself, *"These people are so phony. These people are so empty."* I then heard a little voice down inside of me say, *"And you're the phoniest one of all of them and you're the emptiest one of all."*

Right then, right in front of everybody, probably twenty people, I remember bursting into tears. I don't know if you know this, but that's not right. It's not cool for you to burst into tears when you're a teenager. You're supposed to be in the prime of your life and having a great time. You're the big shot selling the drugs, you're the life of the party and everything is going well. But I just burst into tears.

My friends gathered around and said, *"Ken, what's wrong with you?"* I told them, *"I'm just afraid. I'm afraid because I'm headed for prison. I'm afraid because I'm in so much trouble right now. I'm facing so many drug charges."*

I was lying. Even though I was likely headed to prison and I faced serious drug charges, the reason I was crying was because I was in a hopeless condition. I had reached a place of despair and I didn't know how to get free.

Chapter Three

SPEAKING LIFE
AND DEATH

"Death and life are in the power of the tongue, and those who love it will eat its fruit." Proverbs 18:21 NKJV

Life and death? For something this powerful, I think there ought to be a caution sign on our tongues that warns us to use it with care.

As followers of Christ, I believe it is one of our jobs as long as we are alive to speak life into others. I know that is what I needed in my late teen years. I felt like I would not reach my twenty-first birthday. Even though I was living, I felt as if I was a dead man walking, consigned to the grave and the pit. There was no hope for me. I needed someone who could speak the positive and encouragement that there was life beyond the grave. To this day, I cautiously try to keep a close guard on what comes out of my mouth, especially when it comes to what I am speaking into the lives of others.

YOU ARE HOPELESS

Now, in my younger years, there were plenty of people around me that were speaking into my life, but they weren't speaking into my life in the right way. I remember the first time this happened. I was walking down the street and ran into a friend of mine, who was also a drug addict who shot dope in his veins.

When I came near him, he looked at me and said, *"Man, just go on."*

I said, *"Scott, what's up?"*

He said he didn't want to hang out with me.

I said, *"How come? What's going on?"*

He said, *"Man, you're crazy. You're just totally out of control. Whenever you come around, bad things happen."*

Everything he said was true, and I remember thinking

how pitiful my life had become. Even drug addicts didn't want to hang out with me anymore.

I wish I could say that a drug addict was the only one that spoke that kind of discouragement over me. But it wasn't only him. Friends of mine, dear friends of mine and their parents said, *"Man, don't come around here anymore. You're a hopeless case. You'll never change. You'll be a drug addict until the day you die."*

One day, the pastor of the church my parents attended said to me, *"You'll never change."* He said, *"You're a hopeless case. You're a drug addict and you're going to die a drug addict."* Despair just seeped deeper and deeper into my life because death was being spoken over me over and over again.

Finally, I came to a place that I had to have some kind of help. So, I went into a drug and alcohol treatment center. It was a thirty-day program in a medical facility. It was a place of luxury. They fed us like we were kings and we had our own rooms, our own counselors and our own psychologists. We had our own pool table, and it was just a time of sport for me, except the drugs were absent from my life.

I remember meeting with my counselors and psychologist day after day and they gave me all kinds of tests. They examined me, they discussed me, and they psychoanalyzed me. They tried to give me ideas for the future and give me strategies for living.

And all of this was minus the spiritual aspect of my life. All of this was without Christ. All of this was designed for me to pick myself up by my bootstraps. Even during this, I felt like it was still hopeless.

I had tried so many times. I would try to go without using drugs and wouldn't even make it a day, maybe two. I didn't see any hope of being able to change my life by my own power.

I remember the day I finished that program and went back out into the real world. My counselor looked at me and he spoke these words to me. He said, *"Ken, you'll never change."* He said, *"I've been meeting with you for thirty days and I'm convinced you'll be a drug addict for the rest of your life."*

A short time later, my parents received official documents from the hospital psychiatrist that was in charge of that particular ward.

The documents basically said that I had destroyed my life with drugs and alcohol and that I would never change. They said I would be a drug addict until the day I die and would never be able to function normally in society.

I thought a lot about those words. Those words sunk

deep. When I look back now, I think it all depends on your definition of normal. Many people may still ask if I'll ever be normal, but I'm telling you there is hope. I'm telling you that even when death is being spoken that there is plenty of life.

SPEAK LIFE TO YOUR FAMILY

Again, we need to be ones who speak life to people around us and I think it is especially important that we speak life to our own family. We need to speak life into our kids, our grandchildren, our parents and into our own brothers and sisters. We need to speak things that encourage, bless, and speak to their potential.

There was so much despair and pain in my life with my addictions that were ruining me, car wrecks and fights I was getting into, and being in and out of jail consistently.

One mid-afternoon, I was sitting in a house I had rented with the guy I sold drugs with. He was one of my best friends and we were inseparable. This house was the house nobody wanted in their neighborhood. It was loud with music blaring because of the constant parties day and night. Drugs were always being used and there were always readily available drugs for purchase with a continual flow of people coming and going for those drugs.

On that afternoon, my girlfriend and some other of my

friends were there and by that time of the afternoon, I was so high on narcotics and alcohol that I literally couldn't get off the couch. There was a knock at the door and somebody screamed through the house, *"It's your dad! It's your dad!"*

Now, I didn't go around my parents anymore and anytime I would go to their house, my mom would say, *"Son, we're praying for you."* And this made me feel uncomfortable. I had my life, and they had theirs. When someone yelled, *"It's your dad! It's your dad!"*, everybody scattered. They ran out the back door and my girlfriend hid in the closet because everybody knew my dad. Although he was a good man, he was also a stern man, but by this time, I didn't care anymore. He knew what I was doing and what kind of life I was living.

I knocked on the window, pulled the curtain back, and motioned for him to come in. With the drugs right out in the open and with empty liquor bottles and beer cans right there in front of him, he sat down across the room from me.

Immediately, I raised my voice, saying, *"What are you doing here? Why do you want to harass me? Why don't you just leave me alone? You know what's going on here. Why do you want to come here?"* In my complete dishonoring of his position as a father in my life, he could have rebuked me, he could have reached over and slapped me, he could have done several things that would have been justifiable with the condition I was in. But instead of fully rejecting me, he looked at me and said something that was the starting point of changing the trajectory of my life. *"Son, I came here because I love you. I came here because I just want to spend some time with you."*

Those words sank deep inside of me to a level I did not yet fully understand. I understood my father loved me, but I didn't fully realize then that he was not only speaking for himself, but I believe he was speaking for God as well.

Not only did my earthly father love me and want to be with me, but there was a Heavenly Father that loved me and wanted to be with me. He loved me so much that He gave His own Son for me.

My father came to spend time with me when I wasn't worthy of it and God through His Son came down and hung out with us even though we weren't worthy of it, even though we had rejected Him and spit in His face. He hung out with people just because He wanted to be with us and to restore us to a right relationship with the Father. My father looked at me that day, and I knew he loved me and cared about me. I've never forgotten that moment.

A PLACE OF EMPTINESS

In a matter of weeks, I was sitting in jail again on drug-related charges, still empty and in despair. As I sat in my cell, I heard my name called. I figured it was time for more interrogation. I had been through that many times. The narcotics officer would question me sometimes for hours trying to get information from me and I thought, *"Well, here we go again."*

They walked me down the hall to an interrogation room. I walked in the door, and there was a man sitting there. He had a suit on with an identification tag on, but I didn't even notice who it was. I just assumed it was another narcotics officer, so I sat down. He introduced himself, and he wasn't a narcotics officer. He was the new pastor from my parent's church. The previous pastor had left. He said, *"I'm Pastor Norman, and I just wanted to come and meet you."* We probably spent fifteen or twenty minutes together. He gave me some literature and shared with me how much Jesus loved me, how much the Lord cared about me and wanted to change my life.

I really couldn't hear much of what he was saying because in my mind, I was thinking, *"Why is he here?"* I couldn't justify it. I couldn't piece it together because I thought, *"You know, he pastors a large church in this city. He's a very busy man. I'm sure of that. He doesn't have time to come visit a worthless drug addict in jail. Why would he dirty himself to come down here among us?"*

I wondered if he thought I was a prospect for his church.

Certainly, I was no prospect for any church at all. I thought there were good people and then there were bad people. I believed I was one of the bad people and you never cross that gulf. Once you're there, that's just who you are.

In a little while, we ended our conversation, and he told me he loved me and then he prayed with me. After the visit, I went back to my cell and I remember sitting there just thinking repeatedly, *"Why? Why did he come?"*

It took time, but eventually there was a spiritual application of that. God loves us so much that he'll find us right where we're at, no matter how difficult the circumstance we find ourselves in. In fact, as you're reading this message, I want you just to think about the worst person you know, the one that is completely hopeless. Perhaps it's you. Maybe you've got a situation that's so difficult, that's so hard, that you wonder, *"Is there any answer for me?"* Maybe you have a loved one, a friend, a family member, it could be a coworker, a neighbor down the street or a man that you see on the corner from time to time and you think, *"Is there any hope for them?"* I want to tell you that there's a Father in heaven that loves that man. There's a Father in heaven that loves you. He loves us so much that He came from where we are. He sent His Son to come and be with us so that we could be restored to Him.

A MESSAGE OF HOPE

Even though I was ruining my life, God never gave up on me. On another occasion, after I was released from jail, I had wrecked my car once again, lost my job, and had a girlfriend that was about to break up with me. As I was walking to her house, a car pulled up beside me and the driver rolled down the window. It was a familiar face, a girl named Pat Brewer. She was an addict just like me and we ran around with the same people. I had not seen her for over a year and she looked completely different. I remember looking at her and her face was glowing and beautiful.

She then told me she had met the Lord Jesus Christ and how He had changed her life drastically. I don't remember everything she had said, but I remember walking away astonished. That encounter had such an impact that instead of going to my girlfriend's house, I turned around and walked back to my house.

I went to my bedroom and sat on the edge of my bed. Pat had given me a piece of literature to read, just a message of hope. I remember thumbing through it, not really even reading it, because I didn't need to read it.

It was like a little voice inside me that was saying, repeatedly, *"If I can change her life, I can change your life."*

For the first time, hope sprang up inside of me. For

years, people had been speaking messages to me, and there was power in the words they spoke. Some people were speaking death, but God raised up those who could speak life. They told me, "There is hope for you." They spoke to me and let me know that my life could change. I realized for the first time that there was hope for me. A message sank inside of me that Jesus could change me, that Jesus was my only hope.

I wish I could say that I knelt beside my bed that day and surrendered my life to Him, but I was a very stubborn guy. I continued down that path for another year to a year and a half before I finally turned to Him. But that day I knew that my life could be changed, and that there was hope for me.

Chapter Four

I'M FREE!

There is an interesting dichotomy about freedom. Some claim that the best things in life are free, while others declare that freedom comes at a price. Interestingly enough, both are correct.

I think there are so many things in life that are free, so many things that just come to us we're just able to enjoy. One of the greatest freedoms that I've ever come to know is the freedom from sin, the joy of knowing that I'm forgiven, the power of seeing my life set free. I've experienced that. I know what that is.

While there are many things we get to enjoy for free, it is also true that other freedoms come at a price. The freedom I enjoy from sin that I didn't have to do anything for, the Son of God, the Lord Jesus Christ, paid for with His own life.

He paid an enormous price so that we never have to walk in hopelessness and we don't have to experience the place of ultimate despair. We can go free. I'm so glad that today, I can say, *"I am free."*

Everyone was telling me that there was no hope. My life would never change. I would be a drug addict until the day that I died—I was getting that message over and over again. I was convinced of that inside of myself. But as God raised up witnesses in my life, hope sprang up inside of me.

> *Then I realized something. Jesus said, "Therefore, if anyone is in Christ, he is a new creation; old things have passed away; behold, all things have become new."*
> *2 Corinthians 5:17 NKJV*

You can't beat that kind of deal anywhere. There isn't anyone else that can give you a promise of freedom like that, that you will not only be forgiven, but also absolutely transformed into another person.

A WHOLE NEW PERSON

He didn't just say that I could overcome the hurts in my

past. He didn't just say that I could walk out of despair. He said I could become a whole new person and I can testify today that I am a whole new person.

I look back at my life all those years ago, and it's almost unrecognizable. I think back even as I'm telling you this story, about the things that I walked through, the places I've been, and the things that I've done. I've seen friends of mine die from overdose and others in car wrecks. I've had a gun stuck in my face and it was only a miracle that the man who was so angry with me didn't pull the trigger. The car wrecks I should not have survived. Constantly being in and out of jail. People who considered me a waste of human potential. Every good relationship I could have enjoyed, I destroyed. Every talent, hobby, pursuit or dream was squandered because of my addictions.

But God orchestrated my circumstances, to bring me to the place that He wanted me.

I NEED HELP

There are many times when the help we need is not the help we get. Unfortunately, many times when our loved ones are hurting, when they're going through a crisis, when they're reaping the fruit of their lifestyle, we rush in and we protect them. To this day, I run into this all the time as I counsel drug addicts and their families.

I've watched repeatedly where the family members surround the addict and try to protect them from the negative consequences of their life. They give them money and opportunities and bail them out of jail. They try to insulate them from the pain that their lifestyle is bringing upon them.

HELD HOSTAGE

On one particular occasion, I was counseling with a mother and father. Their son was on drugs and alcohol, and as they told me his story, it sounded much like my story. As we continued talking, I realized these people were totally in fear. Their son was living at home with them and they were fearful of even throwing him out. He had become so unpredictable and so out of control that they were afraid he might actually burn the house down with them in it.

I looked at these people and said, *"You know that you're hostages in your own home. Your own son is a terrorist, and he's holding you hostage right there in your own home. You've created this environment for yourself."* I said, *"You've got to throw him out. Change the locks on the door. Get a restraining order. You have got to do whatever it takes. You're not helping him by keeping him in this environment."* Then I was shocked out of my mind because they told me that their son was forty-five years old.

We do that kind of thing. We try to insulate people. We try to protect people when God is trying to bring reproofs into their life. The best thing that we can do for that person we know whose life is out of control is assure them we love them, and will help them when they're ready to find help. Then we have to pull our hands back and pray for them. We ask God to intervene in their lives. It's exactly what happened in my life.

My parents tried for so long to keep me out of jail and to keep me out of trouble and to protect me. Finally, they came to that place of saying, *"You're on your own."*

I moved out when I was eighteen and for the next two years; I learned what it was like to live my lifestyle–a lifestyle that was out of control. Because my parents made this hard decision, I found out quickly that my life was totally unmanageable.

My parents not only pulled their hands away, but they met with others to pray diligently for me. I didn't understand it, but now I see clearly that God was orchestrating my circumstance. He was bringing reproofs of life to bring me to the end of myself.

I'VE GOT TO DO SOMETHING

After being in and out of jail so many times, it all finally came to a head. I was facing several serious drug charges and multiple DUI charges. My attorney looked at me and said, *"Ken, you might as well face it. They will not send you to jail this time. You're going to prison."* Then he told me to look for some kind of drug program to get into.

My attorney wasn't aware of this, but for four years, my parents had been trying to get me to go to a place called Outreach Ministries of Alabama in Valhermoso Springs, Alabama. There was a man there named Jim Summers. He was the director of that program. He had founded it and he had worked with many drug addicts.

When I was 16 years old, they took me to interview with a man named Steve Hill, who was on staff there at the time. Steve later became an evangelist and missionary, and eventually led the longest-running revival in U.S. history— the Brownsville Revival in Pensacola, Florida. He has since gone on to be with the Lord after a battle with cancer.

At sixteen years of age, I remember Steve shared his testimony, and he wept. As he was weeping, I thought, *"This is crazy. I can't do that. I can't be around this. Grown men don't weep."* Steve told me I would be on a farm for a little over a year with no girls. That's all I needed to hear. I was out the door. I didn't want to go anywhere that there were no girls, and I certainly didn't want to be out on a farm with a bunch of guys that cried. It was just too scary for me.

But as I followed my attorney's advice, I found a long-term drug program in the Atlanta area and was accepted. We made the trip over there and my parents went into one room to interview with some counselors there and I was in another room interviewing there. This program had a very odd approach. Their idea was to tear you down and then build you back up. The counselor immediately tore me down and told me what a horrible, rotten person I was. Finally, I had enough, and I jumped up and threatened to knock his head off. I said, *"If you don't leave me alone, we're going to fight."* I left that room and found out that I was no longer accepted into the program. My parents were devastated. We made the trip back to Huntsville, Alabama.

On the way back, as I was sitting in the car's backseat, it's like somebody flipped a switch inside of me. I had resisted Christianity. I had resisted the church. Many times people had witnessed to me outside of bars or outside of rock concerts and I would tell them, *"Get out of my face and leave me alone."* They must have thought that I was so full of myself, and I was. They must have thought I was so hopeless. Seemingly, that's where I was at, but inside, there was something that knew that was exactly what I needed. Yet I resisted. I fought against it. I said, *"I'm not going to Outreach Ministries and I'm not going to talk with Jim Summers."* However, as I sat in the back seat, I looked at my mom and said, *"I want you to call that guy Jim Summers. I want you to see if they have an opening for me in that pro-*

gram." She was astonished, but she looked at me and made one of the smartest moves that she ever made. She said, *"No, son. I'm not calling him. If you want help, you call him."*

I was at such a place in my life that I was ready to do anything to find some kind of relief, so the next day I called. I didn't get to talk with Jim Summers personally, but one of his staff members took the call. As I shared my story, he stopped me and said, *"I hate to tell you this, but we don't have any openings available."* I said back, *"You don't understand, man. I've got to have help."* He said, *"I'm sorry. I can put you on a waiting list. It's probably going to be at least six weeks before we can find you a bed."* I remember I said to him, *"I can't wait six weeks."* I said, *"Man, listen to me. I'm dying. I know that I will not live much longer. I've got to have help and I've got to have help today."* I guess those are the words that he was waiting to hear because the next thing he said was, *"Well, can you come here Wednesday afternoon?"* I said, *"I can be there Wednesday afternoon."* He said, *"Okay, I'm going to make a place for you."*

Quickly, I called my attorney. I said, *"I found an opening. I found a program that I believe will accept me,"* and he made the right phone calls. He brought me before the judge, and quicker than I could even imagine, everything was settled. I was given a prison term and then they suspended that sentence and sent me into Outreach Ministries of Alabama.

My parents and I drove out to near Cullman, Alabama, where the ministry was at the time (today that ministry is in Valhermoso Springs). They dropped me off and one man began to show me around the farm. I was scared and wondering, *"What is this going to be about?"* I knew the program was over a year long, actually a year and one month long. I walked around and I thought, *"What in the world am I going to do here?"* Then we walked into an area just like a living room. A lot of the men had finished their work assignments for the day, and one of them was playing the guitar. They were all sitting around laughing and talking to each other, and they were singing a song of praise to the Lord. I thought, *"How strange. How weird that guys my age are laughing and they care about each other."* Even though it scared me and confused me, for the first time I felt love. I felt love in that room and I knew something was different here.

COMING TO THE END OF MYSELF

I knew what I needed to do. I had grown up in church. I knew the move that I needed to make and that night I was laying in bed and the Lord was dealing with my heart. I wasn't in a cathedral. I wasn't in a church. I didn't even get out of bed to kneel down.

I just laid there in my bed with my head on my pillow and I said, *"Jesus, if you'll set me free, I'll live for you until the day I die.*"It's as if the Lord was standing over me, waiting for that very moment. It's as if He had been anxiously waiting for those words to come from my heart because for the first time in my life, I was getting real with Him.

I had prayed lots of prayers before. Many times I would be in jail or I'd be in a tight spot. I'd say, *"God, if you'll get me out of this, I'll do better. I'll straighten up. I'll quit doing this. I'll quit doing that."* But I never meant it. It was just an angle. I was trying to con God.

This time He knew, and I knew I was at the end of myself. I was getting real with Him, and if you'll get real with God, He'll get real with you.

At that moment, I don't know how, but I knew I was completely transformed. There were no bells that went off; no lights started flashing, nothing dramatic.

I was still lying in my bed, but peace flooded me, and I realized I was different. At that moment, I knew that my life would never be the same. I was going to live my life from that day forward for the Lord Jesus Christ. I surrendered my heart to Him.

I woke up the next day fully expecting for withdrawal symptoms to begin. I had been through a drug program a year and a half previous to that and went through several days of withdrawals. I had knots in my stomach, flu-like symptoms, confusion and pain throughout my body. I knew what withrawals were. I waited for that to happen, but I didn't have any withdrawals. All I had was peace and joy in my heart. I woke up the next day realizing it had been 48 hours. I just knew those withdrawal symptoms were going to start. They never did.

On the third day, I went to one of the staff members. I was puzzled. I said, *"You know what? I should really go through withdrawal by now, but I'm not. I just feel happy and I feel good."* I remember him looking at me and saying, *"Ken, you've been delivered, man. It's not like the other times when you tried your best to get off drugs when you tried by your own power to be set free."* He said, *"This time, God has set you free. This time He has poured His power into your life,"* and he said, *"You will not go through withdrawals. That joy and that peace you have inside, He gave you that instead of those withdrawals."*

So I came to Jesus because of death. I came to Jesus because of hopelessness. I came to Him when all of my motives were pretty selfish. I was just sick of the way my life was going. But you know what? On that third day, I began to realize that I loved Him. I began to realize that everything I had been searching for I had now found in His presence.

All at once, I realized that even though I came to Him because of death, now I was enjoying life; even though I came to Him with emptiness, now I was experiencing the fullness of His presence.

Chapter Five

RESPONDING TO THE CALL

The first portion of my life was a life of death and addiction. I may have felt the freedom of choosing to do whatever I wanted, but I was a slave to destruction. But after meeting Jesus in 1982, I was set free. Not only free from drugs, but I experienced complete freedom. I now know what it is to live a life of joy, a life of fullness, a life of fruitfulness, to have a reason to live, to have direction. For twenty years I experienced death, and I believed I would never see my twenty-first birthday and, in a very real sense, I never did.

That night, lying in that bed, I cried out to Jesus, and I died to Ken Pounders. I died to my drug addiction; I died to my selfishness, and I died to my rebellion. I died to all of those things and since that night I've been living under Him. I've been enjoying life. I've been enjoying His presence. I've been enjoying having meaning and direction.

HEARING GOD'S VOICE

I've heard many people say, *"I never hear the voice of God."* But He has a way of making sure you hear His voice. The primary way He speaks to us is through reading His Word, the Bible. Another way is through people who are preaching and teaching the Bible, and another way is through friends and family. There are many ways that He can speak, but I found that many times, He speaks to my heart. It's a small voice inside of me and I know what I heard wasn't just my own thoughts. It had more power than that.

STANDING IN MY PLACE

One night, when I was still at Outreach Ministries of Alabama, it came to my turn to share the evening devotion. Now you've got to understand that I was not used to speaking in front of people.

The idea of getting up and talking was terrifying to me. I didn't know what to say. I didn't know how to do that, and I became more and more anxious. One of the staff members finally pulled me aside and said, *"Ken, it's not that hard."* He said, *"I know you're seeking the Lord. I know you're spending time in the Bible. What I want you to do is just take a verse of scripture that the Lord has spoken to your heart, and just get up there and share with the guys what God said to you about that verse."* I thought to myself, *"I can do that. I know I can do that."*

So that night I got up, and I stood in front of about 15 men. To this day, I don't remember what I shared with them, but what I remember is that for the first time in my life, I felt like I was standing in my place. I felt like I had just dropped into that spot that was carved out for me and it was a perfect fit. It was really an odd feeling. Then I remember I heard the Lord speak to me, *"Ken, this is what I created you to do, and this is what you'll do until the day you die."* I've never forgotten that. After many decades of living for Jesus and after almost that many years of ministering in many capacities, I've never forgotten those words.

There have been times I have felt discouraged, and I wanted to quit, but a little voice inside says, *"This is what you'll do for the rest of your life."* Sometimes I wanted to do something else just because this was too hard, but that little voice inside of me, that call, said to me again, *"This is what I created you for and this is what you'll do until the day you die."*

See, I had a plan in my life. I wanted to be a veterinarian. I have always loved animals, and I thought that one day I would work with them full time. Then my life went out of control and lost all meaning, all hope. Now it was restored to me. God gave me new direction, and I had a reason to live. This call came very clearly and very definitely. I realized that the call of God was in my life. I've never doubted that to this day.

From Outreach Ministries of Alabama, I went to another ministry called Teen Challenge International Mid-America in Cape Girardeau, Missouri. I went there knowing God's hand on my life and I had more opportunities to share devotionals again with other guys.

Then I was given the opportunity to be in the Mid-America Teen Challenge Choir. We would travel to churches, to jails, sometimes out on the streets, anywhere we were given the opportunity. We would share our testimony of what Jesus had done in our lives. I remember the altars in those churches were filled with weeping people. They had sons and daughters they had given up all hope for because they were on drugs.

I remember again and again being overwhelmed. I saw how much despair was in the lives of these people. I began to realize that God was going to use my testimony.

Many times when I was in prayer, the Lord would speak

to my heart and say, *"Ken, you're going to preach the gospel all over the world."* I was a young man who had only been saved for a few months. I thought, *"Ken, you're wrong to think that way. That's arrogance in your life. God couldn't possibly use you that way."*

One time, we were ministering in a church in Austin, Texas. After the evening service, a woman of God came up to me. This woman was at least in her early 80s, maybe even her mid 80s and I'm sure that she has long since gone on to be with the Lord. She came directly up to me. There were probably twelve men on that platform, but after the service was over, she came straight to me. She said, *"The Lord spoke to my heart about you, son."* I was all ears, and I began to listen. What was she going to say? She looked at me. She said, *"God's going to use you all over the world. He's going to use your testimony to the nations."* It was an exact confirmation of what I had already heard inside of me. It was just one more confirmation of the call that was upon my life. I just tucked that away inside because I was so young and I thought, *"How could God use me in that way?"*

I finished the Teen Challenge program and went back to my hometown of Huntsville, Alabama. I knew I was going to Bible college. I knew that I would be attending a college called Central Bible College in Springfield, Missouri, but I had about six months before I would be going there.

I got a job, and I worked with Outreach Ministries of Alabama. I began to work with their street evangelism team, just going out on the streets to find discouraged people.

We would go to bars and hang outside in the parking lot. We would go outside of rock concerts, anywhere that people were gathering. We would find people that were hurting and lonely. We would share with them what Christ had done in our lives.

About that time, I met a young lady named Sonya. She was one of the members of the street evangelism team. Whenever I would go see Jim Summers, the director of Outreach Ministries of Alabama, I would see Sonya. She was the secretary. We began to talk and became very good friends.

Finally, I got to the place where I wasn't coming just to see Jim anymore. I was coming to see Sonya, who just happened to also be Jim's daughter. To make a very long story short, I ended up marrying the boss' daughter.

I attended Bible college during the summer. I went directly through and three years later; I graduated from Central Bible College with a degree in pastoral ministry and a degree in Bible. I finished with the highest honors.

What's amazing to me is that before I came to the Lord, many times I couldn't even tell you what I had done the day before. My mind was so devastated by drugs and alcohol that I couldn't even tell you what I had for lunch that day.

Now here I was finishing Bible college, a four-year degree in three years, with the highest honors. I began to realize that God's call really was on my life. He really did have a plan for me, and He had changed my life. I began to realize that He really was going to use me.

GOING BACK TO THE STREETS

My ministry began by sticking a New Testament in my pocket and going back out to the streets where I came from. I would find people wherever they were, people that were hurting, people whose lives were devastated. I would share with them what Jesus had done in my life. So many times I would see people on the streets, and they would weep and share with me what was going on in their lives. God used me to minister to hurting people, and the ministry grew. The ministry developed and doors opened for me in churches, then in jails and prisons, and in high schools. I was amazed!

To this day I have people come to me in churches–many times young men–and they will say, *"I believe God's called me to preach."* Or, *"I believe God's called me to be used as an evangelist. How do I launch a ministry like what you're doing? How do you grow a ministry?"* I have to tell them,

"Here's what I did. I just went out, and I found people that were like me. I found people that were hurting. I found people that were empty and I began to share with them what Christ had done in my life."

Today, we are ministering around the world and God has used us to change lives. When He speaks, you'll know it and the best thing you can do is run in that direction.

Chapter Six

DISCOVERING YOUR DESTINY

DON'T SELL OUT!

I believe that we are born with destiny in our lives, but one of the saddest things is that many people never discover that destiny. They stop short; they sell out. They find what they believe is a little safe spot and then, in many ways, they squander their lives away.

We're supposed to come to a knowledge of the Lord Jesus Christ. We're supposed to find Him. When we find Him, we can begin to discover our destiny.

When I was a child, my folks attempted to raise me in

the right way. They took me to church. They even told me a story about when I was a young child. They were in a Southern Baptist church in Huntsville, Alabama. The pastor preached a tremendous message that evening on surrendering your children to the Lord, giving them to God for His purpose for their lives and really focusing on ministry.

That evening, my parents surrendered in their own heart and brought me forward to the front of that church and dedicated me to the Lord for His service. Later in life they must have thought, *"That dedication meant nothing,"* because of how crazy I got. But looking back, I know they were only responding to a work that God had already done. That's true not only in my life, but in every person's life. God has a plan.

He has a purpose for each individual He places on this planet. Even though my life spun out of control, the day came when I surrendered to Jesus. It was almost like the Lord was using my circumstances and all the tragedy that was coming upon my life. It's as if the Lord was backing me into a corner. He was bringing me into a place where I would discover Him, where I would find Him. I would discover destiny in life.

So one night I cried out, I said, *"Jesus, if you'll set me free, I'll live for you from this day forward."* It's as if the Lord was waiting with open arms; as if He was waiting for that moment to take me by the hand and say, *"Okay, now would you get on with life? You can walk out the destiny that I have for you."*

SET APART

People think that destiny has to do with our predetermination or fate. Usually, this is in a passive sense; there's nothing they can do about it. I believe that definition is totally false. Destiny really means to be set apart. It means that you're set apart for a certain purpose. It means that there is an intention for your life.

Literally, the root of the word means to fasten down, to secure. There's a passage about this in Jeremiah. God was speaking to a young man, Jeremiah, who was a prophet. I believe the call that was upon his life overwhelmed him, about what he knew God was doing inside of him. God used a very direct call to him. He says it in this way, in Jeremiah 1:5,

> *"Before I formed you in the womb I knew you; Before you were born I sanctified you; I ordained you a prophet to the nations."*
> *Jeremiah 1:5 NKJV*

I believe those words that He spoke to that prophet are true in every life, to every individual. When we come to the place that we discover Him, He's free to let us discover our destiny, what He created us for, and what purpose He's built into our lives. He said, *"I formed you."* I know He said that to me. That means there's no accident.

Even though I spent many years living a life that was not only rejecting Him, but slapping Him in the face, all that time, it was in His heart that He had built me for a purpose. He had built within me a destiny. The truth was still there, that He had formed, that He had a purpose and a plan for my life.

Literally, the word "formed" in the Hebrew language means to squeeze into shape, like to mold and to make. It makes me think about what God said at creation, *"Let us make man in our own image."* I believe that image is the life, the divine spark; however, you want to refer to it. God builds something of Himself inside of us. But we are different, we are not God. God is higher, God is infinite, but we are finite. God is awesome, and we are limited.

There is something of His image that's built into us. He's molding us and making us into the people that He wants us to be. Obviously, everyone matters to God. I think about all the years I was out there living in a ditch and running wild; living in total rebellion to my parents and to society. Even then, I mattered to God.

I shared earlier about how the Lord sent witnesses into my life, people to share with me the truth and the hope that was found in Jesus. The scripture says that we, each one of us, are fearfully and wonderfully made. I know the enemy fights against that.

I know that's what was happening in my life. All those years of drug addiction, living for myself and doing what I wanted to do, were really an encapsulation of the enemy trying to bring about my destruction. The enemy tried to blot out that image of God that He had built into my life, trying to end my life before my destiny could be fulfilled.

Scientists say that there are about two hundred and fifty billion stars. Whenever I hear that kind of thing, I always wonder who actually took the time to count them. But that's what they say—two hundred fifty billion stars in our galaxy alone—and there are as many as one hundred billion other galaxies in the universe.

Yet the Lord knows each one of us intimately. That's what the scripture says. He knows Ken Pounders better than I know myself. Even when I was living in rebellion. He knew exactly what He had built into my life.

Scientists say that our brains send messages at the rate of two hundred miles per hour. The scriptures say of the Lord,

> *You know my sitting down and my rising up; You understand my thought afar*

off. 3 You comprehend my path and my lying down, and are acquainted with all my ways. 4 For there is not a word on my tongue, but behold, O Lord, You know it altogether. Psalm 139:2-4 NKJV

We're told that we have about one hundred thousand hairs on our head. The scripture says that He has every hair on our head numbered. So the one who formed us knows us and we matter to Him.

The thing that amazes me even more is that He actually said, *"Before I formed you, I knew you."* He knows more about me than I know about myself. Before I was even conscious, I was already in the heart of God. I was already on His drawing board.

The Bible says, *"He is from everlasting to everlasting."* He had no beginning. He will have no end. So for all of eternity past, God is. Now, that's too big for me. It's more than my mind can comprehend, but that's the truth of God's word. He said that, *"Before, for all of eternity past, He is."* He's God. I've wondered how long did He know me? Before I was conceived in my mother's womb, how long was I in the heart of God? How long was He thinking about Ken Pounders? Was it just for a few moments? Was it for a week or a month or a year? Was it for hundreds of thousands of years? Was it for all of eternity? How long has He been thinking about you? How long have we been in the heart of God? He says, *"Before I brought you out of your mother's womb, I consecrated you."*

This is an amazing concept to me because consecration, although it's a theological word that I think many people don't fully understand, has to do with purpose. Literally, it means to set apart. There's another word found in the scriptures that's related to it–saints, I know that many times we think of saints as people that were near perfection–people that did something significant in the history of mankind, specifically in church history. That's not the biblical concept of a saint. A saint is somebody that God has set apart for Himself. Any one of us that responds to the grace of God is a saint because we are consecrated.

What really sinks into my mind is this; that one night, in desperation, I cried out to the Lord. I said, *"God, please forgive me. Please take my life and take what's left of it and use it."* But that's not where it began at all. According to the scriptures, He knew me before I was born. According to the scriptures, He had already set me apart for His purpose, before I ever came out of my mother's womb.

I think about the words of Jesus to His disciples because they thought that they had made a decision to follow Him. Indeed, they had made a decision. But then He spoke to them and He said,

You did not choose Me, but I chose you and appointed you that you should go and bear fruit, John 15:16a NKJV

I believe that's the tragedy of sin. I believe that's the ugliness of it. I believe that's the rebellion of self will. All those years that I was out there smoking marijuana, taking drugs, shooting drugs in my veins, living in immorality, and doing what I wanted to do. All of those things were horrible enough. But probably the most horrible thing about it was that I was set apart for a purpose. God had set His hand upon me and said, *"This one's mine."* But I was living for myself.

There's a story in the Bible about a king named Belshazzar. It's found in the book of Daniel. Belshazzar was a godless king. He invited all of his closest friends, all the other government officials, and all the most beautiful women of the land to a huge party. They're drinking wine and they're having this huge party. Belshazzar got an idea. He said, *"The gold and the silver vessels that my father, Nebuchadnezzar, took from the temple in Jerusalem, let's get those and let's drink wine out of those. Let's party out of those."* What he failed to realize was that those vessels had been consecrated. Those were set apart for the use of God only. He began to drink and to party out of those vessels. The story goes that a hand appeared on the wall, and it wrote a message on the wall that he couldn't understand. So they sent for Daniel. Daniel read the message. Basically, the message said this, *"You've been weighed in the scales and you've been found deficient. Your kingdom will be removed from you."*

I think about the harshness and extremity of the judgment of God that came upon him. It was all because he chose to do his thing instead of God's thing. He chose to take what was set apart for God and use it for his own purpose.

I shudder when I think of all the years that I wasted in sin and rebellion, in a ditch and in immorality. How I was out there living, assumingely thinking I was just having a good time. What I was really doing was taking a vessel that belonged to the Lord and using it for my own purpose.

Thankfully, God brought me into that place of repentance. It's like in that moment, He said, *"Okay, now I want you to get started with my plan for your life."*

God said one more thing to Jeremiah. And I believe He says it to each one of us. He says, "

> *"Before I formed you in the womb I knew*
> *you; before you were born I sanctified you;*
> *I ordained you a prophet to the nations."*
> *Jeremiah 1:5 NKJV*

The word "ordained" or "appointed" is such a powerful word. Literally, it means I have given you as a gift. I think many people don't realize this. God has gifted us. He's made us to be a gift. God wants to bless each one of us, and He wants us to be a blessing. He tells you that He has appointed you. He has a purpose for your life. He's given you as a gift to go out and make a difference in your world.

Immediately, you think, *"Oh, okay, well, if that's what God did, then I've got to get busy in church work. I've got to preach, or I've got to teach. I've got to be involved in visitation for my church."* All of those things are wonderful. All of those are important things; however, God doesn't divide life into categories like we do. God doesn't see my life as church life one day of the week and real life the rest of the week. God sees all of my life as set apart to Him. God wants me to be a world changer. God wants me to take my gifting and use it out there in everyday life, whether it is as a doctor, or whether it is in the ministry and meeting needs in whatever way I can, or whether I am an engineer.

Whatever gifting there is in my life, He wants that gifting to be released. He wants it to be used for His glory, and for our good. He's created each one of us, I believe, to be a blessing.

Chapter Seven

LIVING THE DREAM

I believe that God's built a dream into each one of our lives. I have talked about discovering your destiny, realizing there is a purpose in your life, that God is the One that formed us. I believe it goes even beyond that.

I have a place out behind my house at the edge of some woods where I like to go pray. It is a place where I can be open with God. I think we all need a place like that, where we can be alone and really mean business, where we can get loud if we need to, not so much for God's sake but for our own.

At my place of prayer, there is a huge, beautiful oak tree. It is absolutely massive. In fact, several years ago in a storm, half of the tree broke away and the half that still stands is still so big you can't get your arms around it. Well, as I was praying, I kept hearing the crunch of acorns under my feet and when I looked down at those acorns; I realized they are a lot like our lives.

Within that one little acorn nut there is so much unbelievable potential, there is the possibility of another massive oak tree and then if you take it further that one acorn that will produce one tree will produce hundreds of more acorns which each have the potential of becoming a tree. If you keep going, that one acorn could produce not only a forest but generations of forests. That is the picture of our lives. We have so much potential, yet we have an enemy, the devil, who wants to keep that potential hidden. The potential has always been there, but many times we fall for Satan's lies and, like the acorn, we never get planted and we lay there on the ground and we die and rot.

That's the extent of what our life becomes. Many people go to the grave having never lived their dream, having never reached their potential, having never pursued the passion of their heart. They decided they would live for safety and comfort, just for a nice little spot that they've found.

There's a lot of talk in our world today about terrorists. Certainly terrorism is a very real threat, and it can be a very scary threat. At the very thought of any kind of terror, many want to find a safe place and hide. While there are many we would call terrorists here on the earth, here is a very real truth: Satan is the master terrorist. He wants to control our lives with fear. That is what the enemy specializes in.

I'm going to go a step further and say that some of his favorite tools are television, the media, magazines and even music. I think about how much there is out there, how much fear we're bombarded with continually. His goal is to have us coil back within ourselves, to draw up into our cocoon and find a little safe place and sell out. We get rid of our dream in favor of having a nice little spot.

THE MOST VALUABLE PIECE OF REAL ESTATE

I've heard it said that the most valuable piece of real estate in any town, in any county, in any place is the graveyard. When I first heard that, I thought, *"What, the graveyard? I mean, nobody even wants to go to a graveyard. How is that valuable?"* Then I realized that buried in that graveyard are so many dreams, inventions, books that were never written, songs that were never sung, concertos that were never composed and cures that were never discovered. The list goes on and on and on because so many people have a dream inside of them, but they never go after the dream.

I think about the story from the Bible where a man named Joseph dreamed that he and his brothers were out binding sheaves of wheat and then his sheave stood upright and his brothers sheaves all bowed down before him. He then had the bright idea of telling his brothers about the dream and they didn't like it. In fact, they already didn't like him because he was daddy's favorite and when he told them the dream, they hated him even more.

He then had another dream, where they were bowing to him, and he shared it with them again. Finally, they had had enough. When they found an opportune moment, they first threw him into a pit and sold him into slavery. After they faked his death and made their dad believe wild beasts had killed him. In their mind, they thought they were rid of the dreamer and his dreams. But Joseph had a real dream. It was a dream that really did come from God. He may have handled it incorrectly in his youthful enthusiasm. It may have come off as arrogance. He may have done it in such a way that it alienated those around him.

In one sense, I admire Joseph because at least he had the fortitude to declare his dream, to realize that God had a purpose for his life. He not only discovered that dream, but declared it and spoke it boldly. The Bible says in Genesis chapter 50 that there came a day where those brothers appeared before Joseph again and the dreams that God gave Joseph came to pass. If you've never read that story, I encourage you to go read Genesis 37 all the way through chapter 50, because it's not just a Sunday school story. It's a powerful, powerful story. It's history. It's the way God moved in this man's life.

THE FAVOR OF GOD

I believe the story of Joseph contains principles that speak to every one of our lives. In the end, to make a very long story short, even though Joseph was sold into slavery and his life seemed to be over, he ascended in power. This was because the favor of God was upon him. He reached a place of prominence and ended up in a household, where he became basically the ruler. There again, he was falsely accused and cast down and he ended up in prison. Even after another let down, he didn't give up. He eventually became a leader in that jail. After a while, two of Pharaoh's officials were put in prison. One was a baker, and the other was a cupbearer. They each had a dream and Joseph, with God's help, could give them the interpretations. One interpretation was good, the cupbearer was to be restored to his position, however the other interpretation was not good at all, the baker was going to lose his head. Both dreams came true and Joseph told the cupbearer when you get before the king, please remember me. Of course, the cupbearer did not remember. After years of slavery, rejection and fear, and all the disappointment, Joseph is still in prison and still forgotten for another two years.

Then one day. Pharaoh had a dream. Pharaoh asked for an interpretation, and nobody could give him one. Finally, the cupbearer remembered and spoke up, *"You know what, king? There was a man in the prison that when I had a dream, he told me the interpretation. I told him I would mention him to you, but I didn't do it. I believe he could interpret your dream."* In a moment, Joseph not only came out of prison, but he rose to a place of authority being second in command of all of Egypt, because he not only gave the king the interpretation of the dream, seven years of great harvest and the seven years of great famine, but also gave him the strategy to store up food to make it through the famine. The king said, *"You're the man. You take the position, and you do it."*

Ultimately, Joseph's dream was fulfilled because the day came that his brothers and their families were starving to death. They came all the way to Egypt because they heard there was food there. They bowed down before this great man, not realizing who he was and said, *"Please feed us."* Little by little, Joseph revealed himself. He ultimately unveiled himself and said, *"I'm your brother."* They must have been terror-stricken, but he was gracious to them. He moved them, their father, and their families to Egypt and took care of them and ministered to them.

The day came that their father died, and those brothers thought, *"Now we're in trouble. It's over. He'll kill us."* They came, and they fell down before him. They said, *"We are your servants,"* which really meant, *"Please don't kill us now."* He said, *"Listen guys, am I in the place of God? As for you, you meant evil against me, but God meant all of this for good in order to bring about this present result, in order to preserve many people's lives."* He said, *"I'm going to be gracious to you. I'm going to take care of you and I'm going to take care of your little ones."* The Bible says that he comforted them and he spoke kindly to them. I think this is such a powerful story because I see a man who lived out his dream.

God built a dream into my life. Soon after I came to the Lord, I would be in prayer and just spending time with Him. Many times I would just get a feeling like a little voice inside of me was saying, *"You're going to travel the world. You're going to go all over the world, and you're going to tell your story. You're going to share what good things the Lord has done to you."*

As a young believer, barely out of my life of sin, immorality and addiction, I remember thinking, *"It's so wrong to think this way."* It's almost like I was beating myself over the head for having a dream like that. There came a day when I realized that maybe this dream was from God.

WHAT IS YOUR DREAM?

I had mentioned earlier that when I was part of the Teen Challenge choir, we would travel from church to church and after one service an elderly lady, probably in her mid 80s looked at me and said, *"Young man, God's hand is on your life and you're going to take His message to the nations."* I remember that was the word that was already inside of me, but I was ashamed to tell anybody.

Several years later, when I was pastoring a church in Alabama. We were reaching out in the inner cities of America. There were a lot of things with which I was involved, but I still had never shared with anybody that my passion was to take the Word of God to the nations of the world.

And then once, when I was ministering in Europe, I was sitting at a little cafe on the North Sea with a missionary. He looked at me and asked a question. He said, *"Ken, if you could do anything you wanted to do, what would you do?"* I looked at him and said, *"I just want to do the will of God."* He said, *"I know you want to do the will of God. Every Christian says they want to do the will of God. But if you could do whatever you wanted to do, what would you do?"* Again I said, *"I just want to do the will of God."*

Looking back, I now know what he was getting at because I meet people all the time that say that, almost like the will of God is impossible to know and too difficult to find. That's not the case at all. In fact, the Lord wants me to know my destiny. He wants me to fulfill my purpose. He wants me to live the dream that He's put inside of me.

The missionary then said, *"Ken, I believe a key to knowing what God's will is for your life is to know what's in your heart."* I'd never heard anybody say that before. Now let's take that a step further. I believe that in order to discover our dream, in order to declare our dream, we've got to be seeking God. We've got to be in a place where we really want to do His will. We've got to be in a place of absolute surrender where our heart is submitted to Him, where we really want to do His thing and not our thing. Then, when we're in that place, we can listen to our heart.

I looked at that brother that day and I said, *"I want to preach the gospel all over the world. I want to go to the nations. I want to raise up churches. I want to equip pastors. That's what's inside of me."*

DECLARE YOUR DREAM

The amazing thing is that as soon as I declared my dream, doors began to open in mind-boggling ways. I received invitations to travel to other nations and opportunities to equip pastors. To this day, we've ministered in twenty-eight nations of the world, *The Conquer Addiction Podcast* has been downloaded in over 100 nations, and doors are still opening into places I've yet to step into.

I believe we've got to come to a place where we declare our dream, where we're willing to say, *"This is who I am and this is what's inside of me."* I believe that when we do that, we also have to prepare for battle. Just like with Joseph, the Bible says that when he told his dream, his brothers hated him even more. When we declare our dreams, there will be other dreamers who support us, but there will be many more dream killers who, whether intentionally or not, will try to sabotage us. Dream killers are usually those who have taken their own dreams and executed them, they have decided that their dreams are impossible, too big, and that they can't get there, after they do that, it's like they are on a mission to make sure no-one else accomplishes their dreams as well. So when you have a dream, prepare for battle and then realize that the key to walking in the dream God has given you is humbling yourself before Him, knowing you need His help.

> *Therefore humble yourselves under the mighty hand of God, that He may exalt you in due time, 1 Peter 5:6 NKJV*

I think about the difference in Joseph from when he

first declared his dream. It was a true dream. It was obviously a dream from God, and yet he declared it with such brashness and even seemingly a little arrogance. When his brothers actually came and knelt before him, in that moment that he could have gloated, in that moment when he could have said, *"See, I told you. Look what you guys did to me. Look how you treated me. I told you that this was the dream, and this was what would happen."* But he didn't do that. When they came to him, he wept. When they came to him, he ministered to them. When they came to him, he attempted to restore their lives to a place of blessing, pleasure, and comfort. When he had that moment that he could have taken their lives, he said, *"Guys, you meant evil, but God was in it, and God meant it for good. God wanted to bring about this purpose."*

It says that the words he spoke to them comforted them, encouraged them, and ministered to them. He fed them and he fed their families from that day forward. He was a different man. He was a different man because of the fear and the rejection, the adversity, and all the things he walked through.

Not so much because of them, but because of the grace of God that was built into his life as a result of his experiences. Humble yourself into the hand of God so that He can exalt you at the proper time. I know that from the time He began to speak the dream to me about going to the nations,

I stored that thing inside because I thought, *"You can't do that. You can't do that."* I know that even while I was walking through difficulties and adversity; I was learning how to humble myself before God. I was learning how to have wisdom.

Ultimately, He said, *"Okay, now's the moment. Now I'm going to let you step through that door."* He had prepared me. He made me the man I needed to be so I could fulfill the mission, the dream that He put inside of me. I believe that's the way that God works.

One thing that impressed me is that Joseph was releasing his gift even while he was still in prison. He couldn't walk in the full dream. He couldn't be all that God had ordained for him to be yet, but he was doing what he could in that moment. I believe that's exactly what we've got to do. So many people have asked me, *"How did you get the ministry that you have today? How did this all happen?"* I have to tell them that it happened because when I first came to the Lord, I just had a heart for people. I had a heart to tell them about Jesus. I would go to the bars, or to the laundromats, or wherever hurting people were gathering. I had a little Bible that I stuck in my pocket. I would go tell them about the Lord. I couldn't do all that He was putting in my heart, but I could do that much.

I don't know what your dream is. I don't know what's

inside of you. I don't know what He's created you to be. It's probably way bigger than you can do. There's that temptation to set it aside and say, "No, I can't do that. I can't do that." I'm going to tell you this: if the dream is from God, it's going to be way bigger than you are. The resources to fulfill it are probably not readily available to you.

When you take that step, when you just begin to release the gift that He's given you, He'll cause the dream to be fulfilled. Don't sell out for less. Don't get yourself a little safe spot. Begin to live your dream and release all of what's inside of you by being faithful with what you can be doing right now.

Chapter Eight

THE POWER OF INFLUENCE

To date, we've had the opportunity to minister in nations around the world, to plant churches in the nations of Eastern Europe, to establish orphanages in Moldova and India. Yet, there is still so much that burns in my heart. I am satisfied with what God has done through my life, but there is still a dream burning inside of me to do more. More with our current ministries and with ministries that haven't been launched yet.

I am especially burdened by the Islamic world, and crossing into Hinduism, the nations of the Middle East and Asia where the gospel has been least preached. That burns inside of me. There's a dream to somehow reach them with the good news of Christ. But in order to reach that dream, I must continue to be faithful with what God has given me to do now. In order to later have influence with the people in my heart, I must be faithful to live a life of influence with those I am currently involved with.

A LIFE OF INFLUENCE

I remember sitting on a plane, headed to Moscow to minister to leaders from all over Russia. I found out later that many of those leaders had traveled by train for days to come to that conference. I wondered, *"Why me?"* I felt like a kid off the streets of Huntsville, Alabama, a kid that was messed up and seemingly had no hope and no direction and would never amount to anything. Here I was going to equip leaders in a foreign land. I thought again, *"Why me?"*

God, I believe, wants to give each one of us a life of influence. I believe we're called to have a life of impact, that we're called to make a difference. I believe that He equips and is equipping each one of us to do exactly that. Every one of us has a sphere of influence. We have people around us that our life is affecting. Many times we don't realize that, but that's exactly what's happening. Our life is affecting their life.

After I came to the Lord, even though I had grown up in

a Christian family, my parents and my sisters were not really sold out for the Lord like they should have been. When I found the Lord, I began to really live for Him, spending time reading the Word and praying; going out and sharing Christ with others. I began to see that it was having an effect on my family's life. One day my mom came to me and told me that even though she had grown up in church, even though she had taught Sunday School for many years, she said, *"Son, I don't think I've ever really made a true surrender of my heart to the Lord."* From that moment, she made that surrender. Then my sisters began to pursue the Lord in a stronger way. One day, one of them called me and asked me for advice about spiritual matters.

Here I was, a young man who had, just a few years before, been a drug addict. It amazed me that they were asking me for direction. That's when I realized that God wants to give each one of us influence. He wants to use that influence for His glory.

I was also invited to come back to the church where I grew up. During my teens, I was a terror to the leadership and to the other kids because of my addictions and partying. They had every reason to never want to see me again, but the pastor invited me to come. He wanted me to speak in his pulpit.

I remember sharing my story that Sunday and it had

a real impact on the lives of the people there, especially on one couple in particular. They didn't know that I knew how they talked about me after I came to the Lord. They had said many times that I wouldn't last, that drug addicts didn't change and that it was only a matter of time before I would go right back to my old life. The day after that service, they came up to me with tears in their eyes and said, *"You'll never know how you've ministered to us. What an encouragement you've been to us."* That had a stirring effect on me. God was using my life. Even though it wasn't me, and it wasn't any innate ability that I had, God had chosen whatever influence I had to strengthen me to glorify Him.

Now we've had the opportunity to train leaders in many parts of the world, to raise up pastors, and even to help establish ministries and churches. God keeps expanding that influence because of me being faithful with the influence I had at that moment.

Jesus said to us,

> *"You are the salt of the earth; but if the salt loses its flavor, how shall it be seasoned? It is then good for nothing but to be thrown out and trampled underfoot by men. 14 "You are the light of the world. A city that is set on a hill cannot be hidden. 15 Nor do they light a lamp and put it under a basket, but*

*on a lampstand, and it gives light to all
who are in the house. 16 Let your light so
shine before men, that they may see your
good works and glorify your Father in
heaven.* Matthew 5:13-16 NKJV

Salt and light are speaking of influence. We're called to
be influential for the Kingdom of God. Influence is being
able to produce an effect without apparent force or direct
authority. It means to have an effect on the condition or the
development of something. I like that definition; to have an
effect on the condition or the development of something.
Another definition of influence is an emanation of spiritual
or moral force.

I like that as well, because I believe that when the Lord
begins to change our lives, then He causes His life and His
power to flow out of us so that we begin to affect people
around us.

I've had some amazing things happen over the years as
I've lived for the Lord. I remember one time I was in Burger
King, standing in line, trying to buy lunch. I was going to
get a Whopper and fries.

A man in line turned around and just began to talk to
me. As we talked, he began to share with me a heavy burden that he had. He and his wife wanted children so des-

perately, but his wife could not get pregnant. The more he talked, the heavier his burden became, and then he wept before me. I'm standing there thinking that this is strange. *"Why is he talking to me? Why is he telling me these intimate details of his life?"*

I realized that it's influence. It's the light of the world, the salt of the earth; it's surpassing righteousness. All these things don't come from us, they come from God working in us and working through us. In fact, Jesus, before He said, *"You are the light of the world,"* He said of Himself, *"I am the Light of the world."*

So there I was in that line, and apparently this man was being affected by something that was just coming out of me. He turned and shared his heart with me. I looked at him and I said, *"Could I pray for you?"*

He said, *"Please do."*

I said, *"No, I want to pray for you right now."*

He's like, *"What? Right here in Burger King?"*

I said, *"Yeah, right here. Let's pray."*

I laid my hands on him, and I prayed for him. When I finished, there were tears streaming down his face. I've never seen that man again. I don't know what happened, but I know that wasn't an accident. That wasn't a chance encounter. I know God was doing something in his life. I know that each one of us has an influence. As we live out who we are and pursue the passion that's inside of us, we discover our destiny and living our dream.

There is life that flows out of our life. It affects the lives of those around us.

BEARING FRUIT

The Bible says that we are to bear fruit. I've thought about that. I've worked around fruit trees all of my life, and never once have I seen a fruit tree strain trying to make something happen. That fruit tree just stands there, and it just draws on the life that is in it. Then it blooms. It bears fruit, and that fruit develops, and ultimately, that fruit is ripe. All of those around enjoy it, and it affects their lives as well. That is exactly what happens in each one of our lives.

We may be near the grave; we may be in a place of total devastation in our lives. We may have dug a pit for ourselves from which we believe we'll never be free.

It may even seem that there's no hope for us, but then we come to that place of surrendering our heart to Christ. We call on Him and He begins to release His life into our life.

As we grow and develop, we draw upon who He is and

His word, and then fruit is produced in our life. Ultimately, we have influence, because those around us look on and say, *"I don't know what it is, but there's something inside of you I need. There's something that's coming from you I'm enjoying,"* and they partake of that.

Early in my walk with the Lord as I was at Teen Challenge, learning to live out my commitment to Him and overcome my addictions, I was housed in a tiny room about half the size of an average bedroom. There were four of us young men who slept in there with bunk beds that had maybe three feet of space between the beds.

Usually we had a pretty good bunch of guys in there, but there was one guy who came in named Carl–he was there trying to avoid prison and it seemed he had one goal and that was to make me miserable. He tested my Christianity continually because he knew I was really trying to overcome some struggles. I really wanted to implement God's Word in my life and he would do everything in his power to frustrate me.

One day I was getting ready for work and I don't even remember what he said, but it pushed just the right button in me. Now, I'm a pretty good sized guy, and he was just a little bitty guy, and I turned around and went off on him. I grabbed him, picked him up, and was about to throw him out the window. Who I used to be, my violence and hatred seemed to come back to me. I shoved him through a second-story window and then I recognized what I was doing and put him down. I then went out and knelt down outside of the room and just wept and cried out to God for forgiveness. I remember Carl laughing at me, and implying that my Christianity wasn't real. He eventually ended up leaving the program. He went on with his life and I went on with my life. Later, after I graduated and eventually met my wife and went off to Bible college, we were living in Missouri and I was in the early stages of my ministry.

One night, the phone rang, and it was Carl. To this day, I don't know how he found my number. I don't know how he tracked me down, but he called me. He had left Teen Challenge and joined the Marines. Something had happened while he was there and now he was sitting in a Marine jail cell and they told him he could make a phone call. He said to me that night, *"Ken, you're the only real Christian I've ever known."* And from there, I had the opportunity to minister to him that night.

I realize it wasn't me. It wasn't some exceptional ability that I had; it wasn't because I'm such a nice guy. It was an influence. It was the life of God flowing out of my life into his life. Even though he seemed to mock it, resist it and run away from it, he was enjoying it and partaking of it. When the moment came, he was ready to receive it.

You have influence. Your life is affecting the people around you. We want to have a life of influence, a life that makes a difference. We want to be world changers.

Chapter Nine

THE CONTINUING JOURNEY

LIVE LIFE TO THE FULLEST!

This life that we live is like a journey, an adventure. As a follower of Christ, there is an ultimate destination, and that is in the presence of the Lord. However, before we get to that destination, we still have a life to live on this earth, and I want to live my life to the fullest. After sidetracking the first twenty years of my life with addiction and heading in the wrong direction, I thought my journey would end at twenty-one, but when I accepted Christ, it was like I was given a new lease on life. God, in His mercy, reached down and helped course correct my life. He pointed me in the right direction, a direction that not only set my final destination to be with Him, but also a direction that gives me the desire and the ability to live my life to the fullest while on this journey here on earth. Only because of God's intervention have I been able to be part of some phenomenal things in ministry and in life. I've ministered in Eastern Europe, Asia, Latin America, and across the United States. We have been able to plant churches, raise up orphanages, and minister in schools, prisons, out in the streets, and in every imaginable setting. Without Him, my life would never have looked like this.

THE FATHER'S HOUSE

One opportunity sticks out in my mind. I went into a maximum security prison in Transnistria, Moldova. Moldova is a very tiny country, about the size of the state of Maryland, and even with it being so small, it is a divided country. After the fall of the Soviet Union, there was a civil war, and the conflict was never fully resolved.

If you go to Moldova today, you would fly into Chisinau, which is the capital. From there, if you travel east, you eventually come to the peacekeepers zone, the demilitarized zone where there are Russian peacekeepers. If you go a little further, you cross the border into a country called Transnistria. They call themselves Pridnestrovie.

It is, in a very real sense, its own country. They have their own government, their own currency and their own flag, but nobody on earth recognizes it. It is like a country that doesn't exist.

I was invited by some of my leadership there to go into a prison where they were ministering. They said, *"Ken, we'd really like you to go in there with us."* It was a difficult situation because foreigners were barely even allowed into this region, much less into a maximum security prison. We made official documents to tell them I was an evangelist out of the church in Transnistria. When we went into this maximum security prison, they told me, *"Ken, don't open your mouth. Say nothing because you're not really supposed to be here."* I told them, *"Don't worry. I'm not saying anything."*

We went through all the stages and eventually we walked inside of the walls of that maximum security prison. We had prearranged for me to meet with the church inside of the prison because there was a man there named Edward. Edward is a three time murderer; he'd been in prison there for about fifteen years and would never leave the walls of that prison because of his multiple life sentences.

About ten years earlier, Edward met the Lord, and his life was turned around. He sought God and spent time in the Word and eventually; he ministered to other inmates there in that prison and led them to the Lord as well. On the day that I arrived at the prison, he had fifteen other inmates in this maximum security prison on the backside of the wall, in a country that doesn't exist, in a facility that I wasn't even supposed to be in. I was thinking this was a precarious situation to be in. If they kept me, nobody on earth would have even known where I was. If they decided to hold me in a cell, then there was not even a U.S. Embassy in that region to whom I could appeal.

It was a very odd situation that I could speak into the lives of these fifteen men. I'll never forget it. As I spoke to them and encouraged them in the Lord, the Lord spoke to my heart. He said, *"This is the biggest moment of your life. This is the biggest moment of your ministry."* I was overwhelmed by that concept, because so many exciting things had happened to me. Yet, the Lord had such value on these prisoners, many of whom would never see the light of day again, in a maximum security prison in a country that's forgotten.

We've had many wonderful ministries in the country of Moldova. A number of years ago, we reached out to hungry street kids in the capital city of Chisinau. We minister to anywhere between twenty-five and fifty kids a week. We feed them, clothe them, give them urgent medical and dental care, and get lice out of their hair. We try to get them into school, and if they'll let us, we try to get them off of the streets. We just want to encourage and minister to them right where they're at. This ministry has been so powerful and still continues to this day. It was really born out of an early trip I took into that country. Another American and I were walking down the street, and a little gypsy girl came up and grabbed me by the leg and began to beg for money.

I looked down at that little girl. She was dirty and seemed so sad. She had pierced her ear with a piece of copper wire and that wire was still in her ear, and had become infected. There was bloody pus coming out and running down her little white dress. Compassion filled my heart, but I realized that even if I gave her the money she was begging for, she would probably never see it. Somewhere around the corner was an adult that was taking advantage of her, taking everything she would get.

With my own eyes, I have seen how these kids live. I have been in the holes in the ground, the basements, the rooftops, and the abandoned building they call home, and through this ministry, we have been able to give them the love of Jesus.

In 2002, there was a young boy named Yuri who came to one of our churches in the neighboring city of Tiraspol. Nobody could find out who he belonged to or where he lived. They noticed that on work days he would show up and devour the snacks that the church provided.

Another time, our workers saw him get an empty can of condensed milk out of the trash, pour a little water in the can, swish it around and drink what was left of the milk. So, they followed him to see where he went. When they followed him, they found he was living in an abandoned warehouse eating out of trash bins. Our hearts were broken about it. How could we say to him, "Come to church, but go back to your home." He had no home. How could we say, "Go back to your family." He had no family. We then asked a couple of ladies to bring him into their apartment and take care of him. With humble beginnings, the Father's House in Slabazea, Transnistria, Moldova, was established.

Not long after Yuri came to the Father's House, we had a little brother and sister come to our ministry. The boy was under two years old and his name was Dema. The girl was about four and her name was Luda. When they came to the Father's House, they were severely malnourished. Their mother was literally insane and their father was in prison. If they ate at all, it was when their mother would throw food out on the floor and they would eat off the floor like animals. They couldn't even speak any language. Apparently the mother never even talked to them. One day, she just dropped them on our doorstep.

As we began to love and minister to them, their lives changed drastically. Our ladies prayed over them, spoke the Word of God into their lives, made sure they were getting good meals and just loved them. Pretty soon they were speaking Russian and then jabbering like crazy. Every time I would come, they would just talk my ear off, even though I couldn't understand most of what they said.

Dema had been diagnosed with leukemia and had a whole series of problems in his little body, but about a year later, we took him back to the doctor. After his examination, they said, *"There's nothing wrong with this little boy. There are no diseases in his body."*

Then, some ladies from our church in Slabazea reached out to Luda and Dema's mom and eventually led her to a commitment to Christ. They began to love, train, and teach her, and more and more, she became a caring mom. Eventually, we had the opportunity to restore Luda and Dema back to her and now they are a happy family. That's really what our ministry there is all about, to see families healed and put back together.

INDIA

Many years ago, we took another step and established The House of Hope in Kalinga, India. It is a jungle region of Orissa, India and life expectancy is very short. We opened the doors with thirty-five kids, which is a little overwhelming to me and all of them were true orphans. They had no parents. Very quickly, we grew to fifty plus children. We couldn't turn the kids away. For a while, we rented a facility and then purchased it. Today the House Of Hope is thriving under the leadership of Vision India.

Why do I tell you all of this? Because God has used a drug addict with no hope of a future to be part of giving people around the world a future in Him. No matter what situation or problems you find yourself in currently, God has a plan for you as well.

Chapter Ten

FINISHING STRONG

One thing that I want to do in my life is finish strong. So many times I've heard people's stories only to hear a very unhappy ending. I want to live my life in such a way that one day when I stand before the Lord, I will hear Him say, *"Well done, good and faithful servant."* Really, that's what every one of us wants to hear.

I think about the apostle Paul. At the end of his life, he uttered these words in 2 Timothy 4:7-8, *"I fought the good fight. I finished my course. I kept the faith. And now there's a crown laid up for me."* I think about Jesus. Even before He went to the cross, He said to the Father in John 17:4, *"I finished the work that You gave Me to do."* And then while on the cross, He said, *"It is finished"* while He was paying the price for our sins.

That's what is in my heart. More than anything else, I want to finish the work that God has given me to do. I want to discover my destiny. I want to live out my dream. I want to exert the influence that He has put inside of me. I want to make a difference in the lives of others.

How do you finish strong? How does that happen? I'm so grateful that when I came to the Lord, there were men gathered around me, and they began to build into my life. They taught me the importance of living a life of integrity. They taught me to seek God. They taught me to spend time in prayer and in the Word. They taught me that above all else; I want to honor and please Him. I believe those are keys to finishing strong. I believe that we need to seek the Lord. We need His strength continually; we need to take time with Him each day to glean from His Word. One of the things that I've found so valuable in my life is to read a proverb for each day of the month and meditate on the wisdom of God's Word. It is also my desire to spend time before Him, pouring out my heart and being still to hear His heart for me. I don't do all of this to check a "Christian duty" off the list, but I want to have a passion inside of me that says, *"More than anything else, I want the Lord to be pleased. I want Him to be honored with my life."*

TESTING FOR QUALITY

When I was a boy, my dad worked as a quality control agent for a manufacturer of airplane windshields. He took me into his test facility one day and gave me a tour. One of the things that so impressed me was some of the tests they ran on those windshields.

One test, in particular, was interesting. They took chickens–not live chickens, but bagged chickens–to simulate birds. They would fire those chickens at several hundred miles an hour towards an airplane windshield. He told me they were testing the integrity of the windshield.

I believe we need to, especially as followers of Christ, test ourselves as well. Now, we don't need to hit ourselves with chickens flying at a hundred miles per hour because that would probably kill us, but we need to constantly test ourselves by asking the questions, *"Am I living out my life to the fullest? Am I who I say I am?"* I can look good in front of people, but am I living a life of integrity? Does my life match who I claim to be, even when no one is looking?

INVESTING IN OTHERS

I believe another key to finishing strong is to reinvest in the lives of others. One of the things that I've discovered over the years is that people are on God's heart more than anything else. He gives each one of us gifts, abilities, personality, humor, and creativity. One reason that He does that is so we can be blessed. He wants us to be blessed, but He also wants us to be a blessing. He wants me to take everything that He's built into my life and reinvest that into the lives of others.

One of the saddest things I have ever seen is a person who is totally self-centered. Their life is all about them, what makes them happy, what makes them successful, even if it hurts others. However, this kind of lifestyle will never give them the happiness or success they desire. In the end, it will leave them many times sad and regretful.

On the flip side, over the years, I've met so many people who pour out their lives into the lives of others and they are the happiest, most fulfilled people. When we reinvest into the lives of others, we give everything that He's given us to the people around us. We help them be the best that they can be.

POUR IT ALL OUT

Another key to finishing strong, I believe, is that we pour it all out. One slogan that I've had in my life from the very beginning is, *"Go for it - don't hold back."* If something is in your heart, and you believe it is from God, then go for it. Take a stand and take action; do it. I want to pour out everything that's inside of me while I'm living out my life on this earth.

I don't want to stand before God one day and hear Him say, *"What were you doing down there? Why were you living for yourself? Why were you so focused on your stuff? Why were you so intent on building your kingdom, Ken? Why didn't you pour out your life down there?"* I don't want to hear those words. I want to hear Him say, *"Good job. You did everything I put in you, and you put it into the lives of others. You took everything I dreamed for you and you walked it out, you lived it out. You took everything that I built into your life and you poured it out down there on planet earth."* That's the way I want to live my life.

There are so many things that are still inside of me. We're ministering, we're equipping others. I want to keep growing. I want to keep developing. I want to be the man that God created me to be.

I'm so grateful for His mercy and grace in my life. I'm deeply thankful for my wife, Sonya, who has stood faithfully by my side all these years. I'm also incredibly blessed to have five healthy adult children and six grandchildren—and to know they will, in turn, raise up their own children.

God has blessed me in so many ways. I don't want to turn those blessings inward. I want to take everything that He's given me and I want to run with it. I want to finish strong for the glory of God and I also want the same thing for you.

NEXT STEP

You may have arrived at the end of this book and realized that you want a better ending to your journey, but have never made the first step in making Jesus the Lord of your life. But how, how does this work? How can we make Jesus the Lord of our life and be restored back to God through Him? The answer to this is very simple. It is as simple as ABC.

FIRST, WE MUST ADMIT.

We admit that, by our very nature; we are sinners. Sin entered this world when Adam, the first man, listened to what the devil said, instead of obeying what God has spoken to him.

> *Therefore, just as through one man, sin entered the world, and death through sin, and thus death spread to all men, because all sinned. Romans 5:12 NKJV*

We also admit that there is nothing we can do to fix ourselves. We need a Savior to free us from our sin.

SECOND, WE MUST BELIEVE.

We believe Jesus died on the cross for the payment of our sins and then three days later, God raised Him from the dead.

> *"Therefore, as through one man's offense, judgment came to all men, resulting in condemnation, even so, through one man's righteous act the free gift came to all men, resulting in justification of life. 19 For as by one man's disobedience many were made sinners, so also by one Man's obedience many will be made righteous."* Romans 5:18-19 NKJV

> *"And He Himself is the propitiation for our sins, and not for ours only but also for the whole world." 1 John 2:2 NKJV*

THIRD, WE MUST CONFESS.

We confess that Jesus Christ is the Lord and Savior of our life. Accepting what Jesus did on the cross is so much more than just a one-way ticket to Heaven when we die. It is a complete restoration to what God intended for man to be. Our model and example is Jesus Christ. That is why He must be the Lord of our life. We look to Him and the life He lived to give us direction and guidance.

"That if you confess with your mouth, the Lord Jesus and believe in your heart that God has raised Him from the dead, you will be saved. 10 For with the heart one believes unto righteousness, and with the mouth confession is made unto salvation."
Romans 10:9-10 NKJV

If you know you need Jesus because of the sin problem in your life, you can pray this prayer now.

*"Lord Jesus, I know and openly **ADMIT** I am a sinner. I **BELIEVE** You died for my sins and rose from the dead. I choose today to turn from my sins and invite You to come into my heart and life. I now, by the grace of God, choose to trust and follow Your leading in my life as I **CONFESS** You as my Lord and Savior. In Jesus' Name. Amen."*

If you prayed this prayer of salvation and commitment to Jesus, I now encourage you to find a Bible believing church to attend and learn more about what God says in His Word.

But now, to end this book, I want to pray over you a blessing.

Father, you know every individual who will read this book and how each one will respond to this message. Father, I pray for transformation and fruitfulness over each one of them. I pray Christ will be magnified in their life and that they would minister the life of Jesus to others. I ask this in Jesus' name. Amen!

Appendix

RESOURCES

- **Mid-America Teen Challenge:**
  TeenChallengeMidAmerica.com

- **Outreach Ministries of Alabama:** OMAinc.org

- **Priority! Evangelism:** Priorityev.info

- **The Well FWC:** thewellfwc.org

- **The Conquer Addiction Podcast:** omainc.org/podcast

- **Calvary Chapel Residential Discipleship:**
  ccbangor.org/crd-mens

- **House of Hope/Vision India:** vision-india.org